Abstract Thoughts of the Absent Minded

Abstract Thoughts of the Absent Minded

A collection of poetry

Rowdy J. Olson

ISBN: 978-1-7378638-0-9
EISBN: 978-1-7378638-1-6

Printed in the U.S.A

"Come to appreciate the wind that blows through closed windows."

-RJO

Table of Contents

Dual Dead

R T
    r
Dual Dead
i   e
n   s
b
o
w
s

Dual rainbows and dead trees
The crows scream and they scream at me
Is it mine to admire, or mine to take?
Do memories exist for memories sake?
Ho ho listen to the crow
As they sing their song to the ones below
There they glare out of a weary eye
Sitting on dead trees as rainbows fill the sky

He whom I seek

Perhaps he is a religious figure as in the book I once read

A being not from this earth is a possibility that was said

But most powerful of all perhaps he is a human mere

And if that to be the case I wish I could stay clear

But tis too late our fates have intertwined

He is the one that my conscious must find

Beauty Past 8pm

The dark clouds stretch across the sky
Beneath the tapestry lies a dark blue
The frozen black flames plastered across the heavens
I realize this is where my heart lie

Bereavement of a Butterfly

With a Broken wing

Here you lie

Unable to return to the sky

I try to help

You run in fear

Losing all that you hold dear

There you rest basking in the sun

waiting for your time to come

Dark Sanctuary

Black church, corroded tree,

what a sad portrait painted before me,

unwelcoming doors, cruel white tower,

your mere sight causes me to cower,

barren lot, empty street,

those inside I do not wish to meet,

but clouds travel, and shadows fade,

churches aren't meant to be seen through shade

The Book

My body watches my soul hang from the rafters

My cold hands skip through blank chapters

Silver Fox

Beware the silver tongue of the silver fox,   she carries no keys only locks

Pernicious Parody

This nothingness I feel
Is that the only thing that is real?
Convince me this is but a dream
Reality held together by a seam
The crude mannerisms of man
Claiming to have the power to damn
Boldly assume what's right and wrong
Always singing the same damn song
The arrogance of man
It makes one laugh
Gleefully

Nature is Bliss

A perfect blue sky on a bright summer day
To thee I can only say nay
But when the sky is nice and dark
Only then can nature win my heart

The Army

An army of none
Will eventually become a army of one
One becomes two
Two becomes three
Soon we are thousands, bountiful as trees
For many a year we will stand tall
But we will drop like leaves in the fall
Our army falls victim to disease, age, and choice
And we few stand proud, proud without a voice
We recall when we were bountiful as sand
Until we die with the death of the land

Fire

The smoke rises to the sky

My heart burns and I don't know why

Why oh why does it captivate me so

As I sit back and enjoy the show

The smoke billows and the ashes weep

Dancing in flame I fall asleep

I awake and there's not but ash

Behold behold the infernos gnash

Cruel

<u>God</u>

It must be fortunate I need decree

That

you

are

still

of

some

use

to

me

Meaning Through Art

Madness fills my soul
My heart bares a hole
Behold behold the laughing skull
Promising to make me whole

13

The Royal Court

the king sits up*o*n his golden throne

eyes bore into t*h*e mAid

hungry to *the* boNe

not noticing the aDviser's *b*lade

the qu*e*en is Inert, not a reason to stir

grown Tired of roy*a*l life

yearning for a knight in shining armo*u*r

to save her from *t*his strife

the prince pla*y*s nearBy

laughing all the whilE

not kn*o*wing their fall is niGh

surrounded by *f*ake smIles

the cook prepares a poisoNed meal

while the bard Sings of better kings

A *s*py breaks the royal seal

wh*i*le the jester pulls the strinGs

the peasa*n*ts are breAking down the door

a knIfe raised,

a pie served,

a mob comes rushiNg in,

all screaming to be free

as three crowns hit the bloody floor

the jester laughs with glee

Fog

I look and cannot see what is directly in front of me.

But I can see with my mind all the things I cannot find.

Birthday Wishes

Three celebrations of birth on one drunken day
People are human or so they say
The drunken smiles fill the room
As they dance a jig one day closer to doom

What is hope?

Black eyes staring down from on high

Eating dreams and leaving not in their wake

Alive but alone

Using their souls

Terrible

Yet beautiful

Social Obligation

With everyday that passes
I grow more distant from the masses

The Buzzard

A colorful surface is what is first seen
Beautiful blue covering the support beam
But out of view is a metallic curse
Sitting patiently from death until birth
Will you let him fly?
You sit and look up, ignoring the pretty hues
Can you see him hidden amongst the blues?
There he perches looking at you.
Waiting patiently to see what you will do.
Will you let him fly?
In a beautiful world he remains starved.
But in a ugly world he does not exist
What part will you allow to be carved?
What will you allow to turn into dust?
Will you let him fly?

Do You Hear The Music?

It's slow
methodical
beautiful
the music that plays inside my head
I must resist for when I dance along I wind up dead

THE IMMORTAL

the reason why He lives searching for love anew, hoping that life's cruel joke be not true, searching searching ever more, ignoring what fate has in store, of all things he hopes to be true, he hopes to spend it all with you, death will come for all but him, cursed to walk alone with his own sin, cursed to watch loved ones die, this hallowed feeling is

Dismal Delight

Is the poet's soul so black and hollow?
True bliss found only when drowned in sorrow
Through pain and fear there is soul and will
And only through death can I find life
To have died yet not be still
To have calmed yet remain filled with strife
So why not laugh till I've had my fill?
Beauty has enveloped my soul and left me whole
And while lost in the dark I've found my heart
The air of melancholy has taken on new beauty
Now neither dumb nor wise I wake with new eyes
Of apathy and empathy or part thereof I know a new type of shadowy love

Simply Complex

Simple souls
Dancing dancing
Simple minds
Dying dying
Simple tongues
Lying lying
Simple hearts
Crying crying

Finite Book

Read you fool read
Cover art from dying artists
Read you fool read
Pointless words on pointless pages
Read you fool read
You really think you can escape?
Read you fool read
Will you submit to the mental rape?
Read you fool read
Covet the knowledge of the sages
Read you fool read
Desperate to find more to harvest
Read you fool read
The book has ended. What will you do?

Dreaming of Reality

I peer from behind broken glass
The curtain lifted for but a moment
Allowing a single cry that would cement
A plea from me for me but not of me
Begging for me to wake up
"Kill yourself." It says
Who do I listen to?

III

Three.

Can't you see.

The meaning it has to me?

The Reapers Pursuit

Run, and run, and run you must,
Running from death from dawn to dusk
He's right behind, you know it well
Waiting to take you straight to hell
Doth ignorance taste so sweet upon thy lips?
Running from yet never turning head
Fearing the touch of bony tips
Thinking if you stop you will soon be dead
You never knew it was life giving chase
Until you run headfirst into deaths loving embrace

Quip

Inadequate. Ignorant. Inept.

Prices learnt and pockets spent.

A fool dancing in place.

Tears trailing down his face.

Devils sought and curses bought.

Importance has lost its meaning.

Will you give one to me?

Imagine

The figments of one's imagination can dream all their own.
What will you do when one escapes their home?

The Jester

Smile you beautiful fool.
Dance a bit longer.
Keep your bell's jingle strong.
Soon the curtains will rise,
and after all this time you will finally know whether it be joke or riddle.

Fear The Flat Character

From the pit of boredom dullness is bred
To be the same when living as you are when dead

The Beast

The beast, it falls

They sing you grand praises

The beast, it fell

Your name will be know for ages

The beast, it's fallen

You're as much a god as God will permit

The beast, it rots

None must ever know it was dead before you found it

The Dogma of Dreams

The reality of dreams
Is that dreams are reality
To be perceivable is qualification enough

Lady Death

Death comes so quickly, she does not blink.
Your barter is pointless, don't you think?

The Merchant in the Sand

He lives in the sand
Trading silver and gold
Once he was young
Soon he'll be old
Dusty hands
Callused and worn
The man of wealth
Faces life's scorn
He looks at his wealth
And gives away his precious stones
A smile on his penniless face
As the desert devours his bones

Cave

Empty, isn't it grand?
To know you are not God
Within there is nothing
To be capable of anything
A being that is perfectly flawed

Niceties

A thousand and one niceties
All sitting in a row
A thousand and one niceties telling you not to go
Look at them and you cannot help but smile
The niceties last for but a while
Dare not look deeper
Leave the curtain closed
You'll find the price is steeper
When you try to face those foes
Face them you must, and face them you will
A thousand and one niceties may offer courage to fill
But when something comes slightly stronger than a breeze
Then perhaps you'll realize niceties are simple novelties

The Beating Heart

Love.

You must see the evil of that word.

Surely you think me absurd.

Love makes the world go round.

Evil is weak to its sound.

Birds float in the summer's breeze

While lovers are brought to their knees

Yet love is meant to end.

A contract with conditions.

The way it must be.

Which is why you must fear the sea.

The boundless sea of love.

From one who cannot feel.

The truest love.

From one who is not real.

The truest love.

From one who knows no right and wrong.

The truest love.

From one who loves all song.

The truest love.

From one who values no life.

The truest love.

From one who feels no strife.

Do you see?

The evil of true love?

Those who truly love do not care if you are alive or dead

Those who truly love keep you inside their head.

The Devil in the Lake

He comes		ever closer.
Can you hear	footsteps	through the water?
He comes		ever closer.
And I am	but	a lamb to slaughter

The Righteous Angels

"We care for all"

"But not them"

"Evil will fall"

"And we decide what is sin"

"Equality!"

"Almost..."

"...necessary causality..."

"...but we don't boast.."

The most righteous stand on a hill

Their heavenly voices exclaim as blood continues to spill

As those covered in blood and tears look up

Hoping for redemption

Hoping for justice

Hoping for love

Hoping for revenge

Hoping for tolerance

Hoping for peace

And the righteous whisper onto them

"Join with me... or cease to be"

Do Fairies Fly?

Can a fairy fly?

                                        Souls so pure we can't comprehend why

Is it destiny? Is it fate?

                                        Who thinks it's their place for these souls to take?

Monsters from the woods take what's sweet and soft

                                        Another fairy disappears from her loft

Beauty is enticing and the Beast can not resist

                                        He does not let go of the fairy's wrist

Deeper into the woods its appetite grows

                                        The fairy cries as the monster's hunger shows

Innocence is taken, by the cruel and lustful beast

                                        Desire now gone, its guilt will increase

The beast leaves the fairy, alone in the wood

                                        Blood drips from a fairy so pure and good

feels heavy and cold, couldn't help but close her eyes

                    she slips away, and this fairy flies

Beholder

Beauty is not judged through the eyes
It is what you see in the eyes
Your decision
Your choice
Let it be known
Let it be shouted from the rooftops
If the world calls you foul
Look in the mirror and decide for yourself

Magic Mirror

Mirror, mirror, oh shattered mirror
Conjure that image that brings me fear
Bring forth your devils
Your imps
Your monsters aplenty
Conjure your horrors on the count of three
One.

Two.

Three.

There it is, the demon of the mirror
That damnable creature that brings me such fear
I look and feel such appall
As I stare in a mirror that holds no magic at all

Reputable Reprobate

Am I villain by nature
Or perhaps it was learnt
Why is there such allure
Such desire to be burnt
For what reason does she call
The seductive voice in the dark
Would I scale that wall
When she only wants my heart
Her voice never demands... only whispers in the breeze
Her words blanket me... promising such sweet niceties
Shake her from my mind
And shake her from my heart
I will not know my kind
I will learn to fear the dark

Wollahs

Simple thoughts for such complex minds

Have you seen what rests inside?

All that is known is little less than enough

Love itself cannot light a candle that will not snuff

Longing for something else... something deeper...something more....

Open your eyes and realize your heart's an open sore

When is not enough finally enough?

Metal Coffin

Death threatened to come near again today
But decided that I should stay
Through twisted metal do I crawl
The end to my story apparently is something to stall
Care not for the trivial, life begins anew
So many things I wish to do
Black, and white, and the grey in between
The world is a tapestry and I hold the seam
Hold your hand, I will no longer
It is not yours to decide when I will be somber
My darkness is light, and light is dark
Beware when the soulless open their heart
Woe my friend. Allow me to love you so
And realize love is temporary as I decide to let go

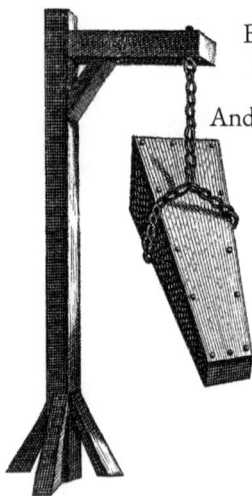

Doppelganger

He dances ever closer.
He who rests within.
His face is like a poster.
The embodiment of sin.
Fear him to no end.
He who dances to the song.
Fear he who will transcend.
Who loves both right and wrong.

Stand and Deliver!

Stand and Deliver!

Give all you have to me!

I have earned it, have I not?

I mean, it's clear to see

If our roles were reversed

Which, mind you, is completely perverse

You would say a line rehearsed

demand my coin filled purse

And upon my refusal I would be soon in a hearse

So, give me my due, I have no intention to screw

My justification is as justifiable as justice will allow

So stand and deliver!

And give me all you are right now

Else... end up a red stain

Upon this walkways dirt

It is not my pleasure to maim

But I do know how to hurt

Stand and deliver, fair woman!

Oh what an honor it must be

For a lowly creature such as you

To be robbed by one like me

Now reach into your purse

And retrieve for me my worth

Don't assume my value too low

And on our separate merry ways we go

A gun in your purse!

My goodness how perverse!

You've just pulled the trigger!

Please go fetch me a nurse!

Oh such a highwayman to be fellen by a cur

Oh dear... my vision has begun to blur

Amongst all my villainy this is surely a first

It seems next time I rise it will be into a hearse

Stand and deliver

You've taken all I am

Sit and collect

Now I'm buried beneath the sand

Of Love

Care I must, care I will

I will love you,

but within my own definition of love

not the one forced upon me by the heartless,

the soulless,

and the empty

Hunger no longer, because I am the latter

Please.

Eth

Path - *os*

<u>*Log*</u>

Numb minds fill the air

Demanding that you care

Their world burns but yours already burnt

No more ashes now only dirt

When constructing yourself anew

Don't allow the others to tell you what to do

Mind Games

Lies

Lies

Nothing but lies

Knowing they'll lead me to my demise

I still spill them all the same

To die playing this game

Of Hunger and Beauty

A mind deprived of its desire
Ignores that desire is a liar
Lost in the fog
Hungry as the dog
See one's morals go up in a fire
With desired achieved
Aware you were deceived
Long past the point of relief
The laughter rings
It's him again
The devil sings
It's time to sin

No Vacancy

Help.

My mind.

Numb once more.

Heavy.

My limbs.

I am sore.

Hungry.

My heart.

Just a whore.

Hateful.

My hands.

Covered in gore.

Happy.

My soul.

Washed onto shore.

Helpless.

My body.

Falls to the floor.

E
Ec
Ech
Echo
cho
ho
o

Numb thoughts echo within the skull

Day in

Day out

Difficult to maintain the role

But the audience has come to see a show

The curtains must be drawn

Is it so rude to demand for intermission?

Though even I admit it's gone on for too long

Laugh and cry

Time to wake up

Time to dream again

Why not demand a full cup

Why not realize it is time to begin

Don't become stuck in the vices of reality

For they will make you as trivial as them

Look into nothing and start to see

Find something of your own to succumb

The (Immoral) Moralist

The immoral moralist stands tall, despite his hunched back
Feasting on others to account for qualities therein lacked
The grin portraying perfect straight teeth hides a blackened tongue
Blind damnation, due to limitation, sounds no better when sung
The immoral moralist heckles loudest, from the stands or in the street
Despite your humanity he only sees stale meat
An appetite has grown, from within his rotting gut
Willing to push you down if only to justify his strut
You have no name, you are no one, and will amount to nothing
Now lay down and shut up while the bloodied angels sing

Bloody Feet

A beauty dances
Through broken glass
Though her feet bleed
She still has such class
The moon watches alone
As the bell tolls
For an audience of one
Her feet fill with holes
Alone she is not
This candle will not snuff
She has herself
Which is more than enough
The glass is nothing
As she dances evermore
Her will is her fire
As she dances on the shore

Small Moments
Small moments
Into forgotten memories
Until a single second
A single moment
A single snapshot surfaces
And that small moment means more than all the big ones combined

Lost Moments
Lost moments
Wrongly spent
Hold me a moment longer
So that I may cry into your shoulder
Am I not strong?
Certainly I tried
Try harder
Savor the lost moments
Grab hold,
And never let go

Grains of Sand

.

Count to one
It's said and done
My life is yours no more
Count to three
It's clear to see
What fate has in store
(Not for me but you
Consider what you'll do)
Count to five
Long past alive
You hit the bedroom floor

.

Feast

Emotion is my meal
I cannot go without
It's what I love to steal
To quench my eternal drought
Hunger, hunger, hungry still
To eat until I've had my fill
My plate is nearly empty
Who will fill it next?

The Necromancer

Words of praise

To raise the dead

Weep for the forgotten

On memories they graze

To find words unsaid

The revenge of those within

Doors 1 & 2

Test the fates

See what Lady Luck has in store for you

Pick door number one?

Or door number two?

Life hinges on blind luck

There are no such things as lies

But even so you must surmise

luck is but chaos in disguise

Are you not a creature of chaos?

Born from blind chance

Born from nothing there is no loss

You have no choice but to advance

Now make a choice because you know it's all the same

Behind both doors you'll find the nothingness from which you came

ABOUT AUTHOR SECTION

Rowdy Olson is a young author, authentic auctioneer, and an award winning videographer. He has been influenced by a unique combination of new and old age horror authors (including R.L Stine, Christopher Pike, and Robert Bolch), long dead philosophers (including nihilists, optimists, and old men who never shaved), and comedic groups (such as Abbott and Costello, Marx Brothers, and Red Skelton). All this while living in the desert southwest and having access to the entire world through the internet has resulted in a unique writing style that can boast both humor and horror. With several projects in the works, we cannot wait to see what the future will bring forth.

Website: www.RowdyJOlson.com

Instagram: RowdyOlson

Facebook: Rowdy J Olson